Yes!

When I ask,
sometimes I hear "**yes**,"
and sometimes I hear "**no**,"
and that's okay!

When a friend
says "no,"
I listen and give
them space—
I am kind!

NO!

Stop means
STOP!

I can play
and still give
space—yay!

I'm kind when I give
my friends space!

"Please don't touch!" keeps me and my friends safe!

I keep my hands
to myself when
waiting in line—
it's my secret
power!

I respect my space,
and I respect yours too!

I keep my
hands to myself.
I know my
boundaries!
The End!

My Amazing Toddler Behavioral Series

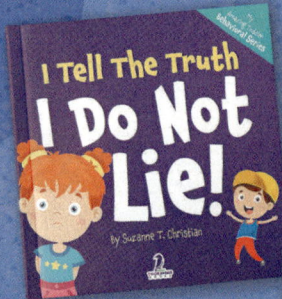

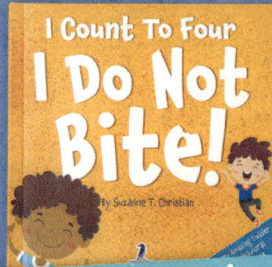

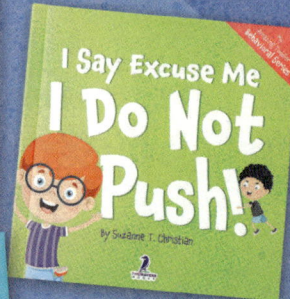

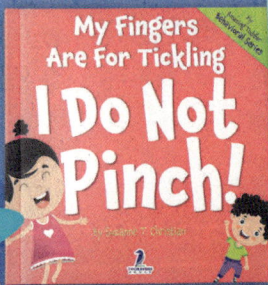

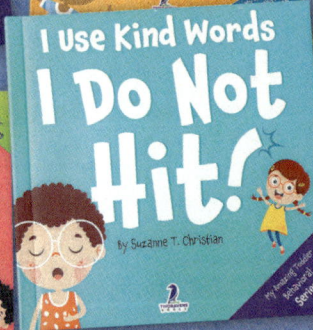

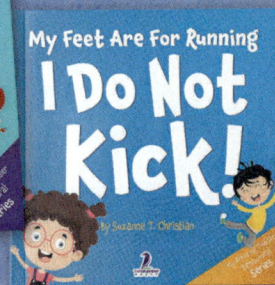

I Tell The Truth
I Do Not Lie!
by Suzanne T. Christian

I Count To Four
I Do Not Bite!
by Suzanne T. Christian

I Say Excuse Me
I Do Not Push!
by Suzanne T. Christian

My Fingers Are For Tickling
I Do Not Pinch!
by Suzanne T. Christian

I Use Kind Words
I Do Not Hit!
by Suzanne T. Christian

My Feet Are For Running
I Do Not Kick!
by Suzanne T. Christian

Check Out
Suzanne T. Christian's beloved series
'My Amazing Toddler Behavioral Series'.
Young readers are sure to enjoy!

Two Little Ravens
CHILDREN'S NON-FICTION BOOKS

Dear Amazing Reader,

Thank you for diving into **I Keep My Hands to Myself. I Know My Boundaries!** with me. If this book touched your heart or made a difference for a young reader, I'd be grateful if you could share your thoughts in a review. Your feedback inspires my future work and helps others discover the magic within these pages.

I'd love to hear from you directly if you have suggestions or ideas for improving the book. Please feel free to reach out to me at **suzanne.christian@tworavensbooks.com.** Your voice counts, and I cherish it deeply.

With heartfelt gratitude,

Suzanne

Made in the USA
Las Vegas, NV
05 February 2025

Modern South Korea

Fasten your seatbelts, because we're about to zoom into the exciting world of modern South Korea! This is a country that's always on the move, creating cool gadgets, catchy music, and unforgettable movies. Let's explore how South Korea has become a powerhouse of innovation and pop culture.

A Tech-Savvy Nation: Gadgets and Industries

Imagine a place where robots help out in restaurants, cars drive themselves, and you can control your home with just your voice. Welcome to South Korea, one of the most technologically advanced countries in the world! Companies like Samsung and LG are famous for making smartphones, TVs, and other gadgets that people use every day. South Korea is also a leader in industries like automobile manufacturing and shipbuilding. It's a country that loves to invent and create, always looking for the next big thing in technology.

The Wave of Pop Culture: K-Pop, Dramas, and Movies

Now, let's dive into the colorful world of South Korean pop culture. Have you ever heard of K-pop? It's a style of music that's taken the world by storm, with bands like BTS and BLACKPINK leading the charge. K-pop is known for its catchy tunes, impressive dance routines, and fashionable outfits. It's not just music; it's a global phenomenon!

But there's more to South Korean entertainment than just K-pop. Korean dramas, also known as K-dramas, are TV shows that have won the hearts of viewers around the world. With their intriguing storylines and relatable characters, K-dramas like "Crash Landing on You" and "Squid Game" have become international hits.

And let's not forget about movies! South Korean cinema has gained worldwide recognition, with films like "Parasite" winning prestigious awards and wowing audiences with their storytelling and creativity.

South Korea on the Global Stage:
The Olympics and Beyond

South Korea has also made its mark on the world stage through events like the Olympics. In 2018, the city of Pyeongchang hosted the Winter Olympics, showcasing South Korea's hospitality and its ability to put on a spectacular show. From the dazzling opening ceremony to the thrilling sports events, the Pyeongchang Olympics were a proud moment for South Koreans.

But the Olympics aren't the only way South Korea has shined globally. The country is also known for its contributions to science, diplomacy, and efforts to promote peace and cooperation around the world.

Modern South Korea is a place of endless possibilities, where tradition meets innovation, and where creativity knows no bounds. It's a country that's always looking forward, dreaming up new ideas and sharing its vibrant culture with the world. So, if you're ever in South Korea, get ready for an adventure that's as exciting as the latest K-pop hit!

The Best Places to See in South Korea

Get ready for an adventure and make sure to bring your camera, as we embark on a journey to discover some of the most incredible sights in South Korea! From the lively streets of Seoul to the serene allure of Jeju Island, there's a whole world of wonders waiting to be explored. Let the adventure begin!

Seoul: The Heart of South Korea

Seoul is not just the capital city; it's the heartbeat of the country. Imagine a city where towering skyscrapers meet ancient palaces, and where every street is filled with energy and excitement. One of the must-visit places in Seoul is Gyeongbokgung Palace, a stunning example of traditional Korean architecture. It's like stepping back in time to the days of kings and queens!

For a taste of modern Seoul, head to Myeongdong, a shopping paradise where you can find everything from trendy clothes to delicious street food. Don't forget to try some Korean snacks like tteokbokki (spicy rice cakes) and hotteok (sweet pancakes)!

Jeju Island: A Natural Wonderland

Next, let's fly to Jeju Island, a magical place with waterfalls, beaches, and volcanic landscapes. One of the island's wonders is the Jeju Volcanic Island and Lava Tubes, a famous UNESCO World Heritage site. You can explore caves formed by lava and feel like you're on an adventure in a fantasy world.

Jeju is also famous for its beautiful beaches, like Hyeopjae Beach, where the sand is as white as snow and the water is crystal clear. It's the perfect spot for building sandcastles or just relaxing by the sea.

Gyeongju: A Journey Through History

If you love history, you'll be amazed by Gyeongju, a city that's like a giant outdoor museum. Here, you can visit Bulguksa Temple, a masterpiece of Buddhist art, and Seokguram Grotto, a cave temple with a giant Buddha statue. Walking through these ancient sites, you'll feel like you've traveled back to the time of the Silla Kingdom.

Busan: A Coastal Gem

Last but not least, let's head to Busan, a city known for its stunning coastline and delicious seafood. Haeundae Beach is the place to be for sun, sand, and sea. It's one of the most popular beaches in South Korea, and it's easy to see why! Don't miss the Jagalchi Fish Market, where you can see different kinds of sea creatures and try some of the freshest seafood you'll ever taste. It's a feast for the senses and a great way to experience the local culture.

South Korea is a country full of wonders, from its vibrant cities to its impressive natural beauty. Whether you're exploring ancient palaces, relaxing on beautiful beaches, or discovering historic treasures, there's always something new and exciting to see. So, let your curiosity lead the way and enjoy every moment of your journey through South Korea!

South Korea's Future

The future looks bright for South Korea, with big plans in technology, science, and taking care of our planet. It's a place where young people like you can dream big and make those dreams come true. And guess what? Your adventure with South Korea doesn't have to end here! There's so much more to discover, from yummy Korean food to learning the Korean language. Who knows? Maybe one day, you'll be part of South Korea's incredible journey into the future. So, stay curious, keep learning, and let's see where the adventure takes us!

Visit our author page for more children's books,
and remember to follow us for updates on new releases,
including illustrated storybooks, biographies,
fun-fact books, coloring books for kids, and more:

Amazon.com/author/88

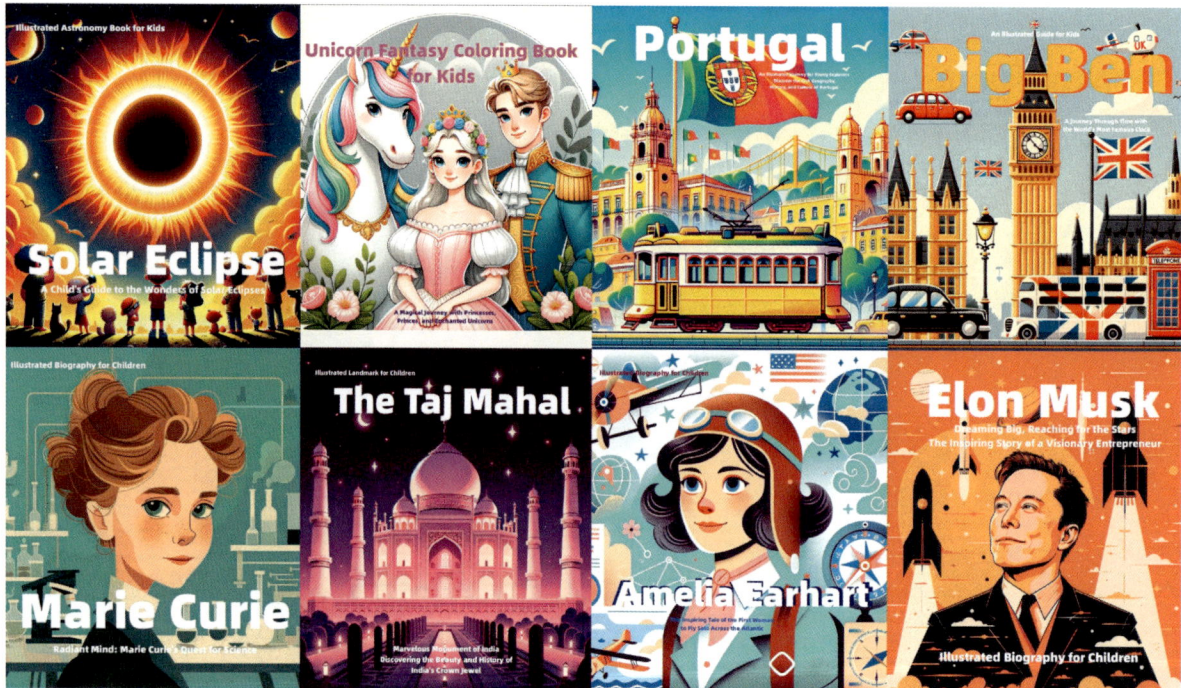

17611187R00026